Is That All There Is?

Margaret Eddershaw

Is That All There Is?

Is That all There Is?
published in the United Kingdom in 2017
by Leslie Bell trading as Mica Press
47 Belle Vue Road, Wivenhoe, Colchester, Essex CO7 9LD

www.micapress.co.uk | books@micapress.co.uk

ISBN 978-1-869848-16-3
Copyright © Margaret Eddershaw 2017

The right of Margaret Eddershaw to be identified as the author of this work has been asserted by her in accordance with the Copyright, Designs and Patents Act of 1988.
All rights reserved.

No part of this book shall be reproduced or transmitted in any form or by any means, electronic or mechanical, including photocopying, recording, or by any information retrieval system without written permission of the publisher.

Cover design by Les Bell.

Photograph of painting on cover:
'Varuna CK442' by James Dodds,
© James Dodds 2017.

For Joseph, Charlie, Mo, Skander, Silas

Acknowledgements are due to:

Artemis Poetry
Blue Chrome Poets
Early Works Press
Envoi
Excel for Charity
King's Lynn Literary Festival
Lancaster Literature Festival
Loose Muse
Petra Kenney Prize
Poetry Space
Ragged Raven Press
Seam
The Red Shed
Ver Poets
The Virginia Warbey Prize.

Contents

LEAVING FOOTPRINTS … 1
   Hanging Over Rio … 3
   Lucy in the Sky … 4
   Sweet Sitar … 5
   Bai Tho Non La (Poem of the Conical Hat) … 6
   Baggage … 7
   The Coat … 8
   Meeting of the Waters … 9
   Cedars … 10
   Walking Java's Rice-fields … 11
   Exchange … 12
   Museum Whispers … 13

WINE-DARK SEA … 15
   Humpback … 17
   The Net-shed … 18
   Heart of Oak … 19
   This Water … 20
   Lobsters … 21
   Ana's View … 22
   All at Sea … 23
   Up Close and Personal … 24
   Scattering … 25

FREE SPIRITS … 27
   Galapagos Heron … 28
   The Pianist … 30
   Arctic Trees … 31
   Nest … 32
   Buphagus … 33
   Wings … 34
   Narcissus at the Window … 35
   Flower of Love … 36

HAPPY FAMILIES … 37
   Udaipur Pulse … 39
   Folding Sheets … 40
   Forgetting the Lines … 41
   Offbeat Concerto … 42
   Happy Families … 44
   Mimosa … 45
   Sunday Stones … 46
   Stuff … 47

Leaving Footprints

Hanging Over Rio

Run
run down a jutting platform
at five thousand feet
eyes on the horizon,
bold as a fledgling leaving its nest,
run into space
till weightless.

Thermal over
Rio's rainforest lungs
that heave and bunch
like green coral in limpid water,
crowding colonial facades,
legoland skyscrapers,
hotels with roof-gardens and winking pools.

Arms outstretched
soar like Christ the Redeemer,
who gazes at the shrine
of Maracana Football Stadium,
while a scramble of *favelas* at his feet
is poised to mudslide
onto unequal neighbours.

Glide out to embrace the misty bay,
turn for a homing pigeon's view
of city patchwork,
sigh down, down,
soft as a feather in a draught,
to leave footprints
in Copacabana's caster sugar sand.

Lucy in the Sky

On seeing 'Lucy' in the National Museum of Ethiopia

Moist white hands
scratch like hyenas
for fragments
in Homer's land of 'burnt faces',
lung-searing heat
volcanic dust
glare of rock
shin   vertebra   tibia
dig deeper
gathering excitement
retreat to camp
jigsaw the pieces,
as a tape plays the Beatles'
Lucy in the Sky with Diamonds.

Forty years on
the pale copy of her skeleton
lies under cool glass,
an adult female
height of a modern child
innocent as all unfleshed bones;
symmetrical ribs stitch themselves
onto a beaded tapestry,
thread this three million year old
on a double twisted chain
to reach us
weave her into our world picture.

The small skull with protruding jaw
chimplike
yet she had human teeth.
One femur joined to pelvic bone
proves her bipedal,
the other detached leg dances;
cause of death unknown.
Lucy's last act:
foraging for crocodile eggs.

Sweet Sitar

One sole cradles the sitar bowl,
the other beats time into coir,
he coaxes his recalcitrant sitar
into showing off: their symbiotic
shadow looms up a rear wall,
as soaring scales entwine,
lure listeners into ancient mazes.

A woman strokes her tanned feet,
two students inhale pot,
a local man slaps his thigh
in ostentatious accord,
silk folds of a melodic saree
ravel and unravel, thread me
to the polished belly of harmony.

Sweat pearls adorn the sitar player,
ornate notes carry on cushions of air
towards the dying light, as though
he touches multiple salvation
with his bare fingers, and time revolves
into yesterday on the hinge of incensed
music, evoking my first hearing

of 'Sergeant Pepper' and George's ghost
sits quietly at the sitar's shoulder;
long fingers pause and his moustached
smile hovers, reaffirming that love
could still save our world,
before vanishing lip by lip,
leaving life to flow on and on.

Bai Tho Non La (Poem of the Conical Hat)

In the Vietnamese city of Hué, during dangerous times, poets wove poems into their hats. These could be read by holding them up to the light.

Once I watched for B52s,
scuttled like a roach
from toxic sprays
bomb-blasted into scorching air,
or fell spinning in death's dust.

Now I follow
the mud-sheened buffalo
ploughing fields of mirrors
bend to plant and plant and plant
shoots verdant with life,
shield the baby from sun
shelter mother in steamy rain,
glide in a boat, poled along
slow-moving rivers of sepia,
weave among scurries of bikes
laden with squirming pigs,
bounce and bounce above the yoke
balancing luscious fruit,
squat in a restless sea
of identical hats
selling mosaics of fish
ducks and fresh-picked greens
(though Vietnamese say
two women and one chicken
make a market).

But in imperial Hué
I am more than practical,
with poems of pain and protest
of celebration and love,
woven between secret layers of palm,
brought to sunlight
like kaleidoscopes of hope.

Baggage

Ellis Island Museum has a display of luggage left by some of the immigrants that passed through between 1892 and 1954

A high-rise of abandoned luggage
imitates the fabled city:
polished mahogany trunks
with domed tops and metal trim
line up like brownstone houses,
next to tooled-leather suitcases
and piled packing-cases
shabby as tenements.

They whisper of flight
from hunger, war, persecution,
of savage seas and stinking holds,
how they kept safe
those precious papers,
best clothes,
favourite cooking-pots.

Some chuckle
at their owners' refusal
to stow onboard baggage,
clinging to case, basket or carpet-bag
like a talisman.
Now they are a ghost town,
their contents borne away
in search of the rainbow's end.

The Coat

*Chinese legend tells of a woman taking a winter coat to
her husband, press-ganged to work on the Great Wall.*

Three months since cherry blossom
drifted like snowflakes
onto my red silk wedding-dress
and whips and horses
took him at dawn,
three months carrying his seed.

He has no coat for winter,
so its bundle on my back
I confront village stares
women spitting contempt
children throwing pebbles
as at a stray dog.

Before me, the Emperor's stone dragon
winds its tail through trees,
I climb steep, uneven steps
between walls topped with huge teeth
up to a watch-tower in swirling mist,
the dragon breathing over the world's edge.

Weather-beaten faces gather
I show my bundle -
there are murmurs of mudslides,
workers falling into the ravine,
they shrug -
my child is heavy as granite.

I wrap myself in his coat
sink against walled roughness
through cracks, wind whistles notes
from his bamboo flute
snowflakes drift onto the coat
like cherry blossom.

Meeting of the Waters

Cooler, creamy Amazon
meets coffee-coloured Negro
to samba together
in a fringed skirt
six miles before blending -
like Brazil's different beauties -
in the tumult
of life's currents:

black caimans air
smiling profiles,
copper turtles nose
through cloying mud,
pink dolphins breach
to blow fountains,
piranhas flaunt
the white teeth of privilege.

Cedars

Our fragrant forest
once shaded all Mount Lebanon,
but pharaohs, kings, knights, sultans
battled over this crazy crossroads:
plump buds blackened,
saplings withered,
men fell like pine-needles in layers of loss,
so the mighty could mark this soil
with their footprints.

Stories of men demanding fruit
before blossom fades
whisper from leaf to leaf,
reach us in the cries of red kites;
and conflict comes round like seasons,
as though our forest were lopping
its own limbs from life.

Down there, Beirut's new buildings
are planted beside war-torn tenements,
pockmarked as diseased boles,
curtains fluttering at sore-eyed windows
like trapped birds of prey,
or gaunt ghosts that haunt the living
with past mistakes.

Cedars are still the native breath
of resistance here,
our roots are firm and hearts strong,
snow will come soon
to shroud these boughs
in impermanent peace,
while the militias wait.

Walking Java's Rice-fields

Emerald fields of rippling silk
embrace the silver trickle of water,
like an Indian bedspread
dancing with miniature mirrors;
wayward palms lean
to garner rice-leaf whispers
and paths slide from stone
to grass to mud
then resolve into plank bridges.

Passers-by spread smiles
broad as their conical hats
or shade shyness
under the slanted brim;
one is half-hidden
by a shoulder of straw,
another gathers his harvest
of coconuts that float downstream
like severed heads.

In three hours my footfall absorbs
this landscape's ancient patterns
and the verdant peace
of its intimately divided space
transports me
to forgotten parts of myself:
as if being displaced here
gives me the freedom
to re-plot my inner map.

Exchange

A bonsai Rajasthani woman,
pleated into a shimmering saree,
shapes cow-dung
into a small circle,
then presses it onto her house-wall
to join neat lines of others
drying in the sun,
her movements precise and elegant
as Indian classical dance.

I show her my camera,
seeking permission for a photo,
and she poses
against the patterned background
as though in a wallpapered room,
cow-pat in hand,
overshone by her smile.

She accepts my grateful coins,
then plucks six dry discs,
puts them in a black, plastic bag
and gives it to me,
satisfied
that now I have fuel
to cook my next meal.

Museum Whispers

On visiting the Hyde Park Barracks Museum, Sydney.

Through fissures in time
I caught her icy breath, knew her shame
as she was dragged from gaol,
a man's jacket over the flannel petticoat,
to be cargoed on her first ever boat,
with women shrieking like rats in a pail.

She took my hand and I felt her callouses,
she whispered, as we creaked upstairs,
of the terrible heat as they landed,
a pasty English soldier in arrogant red
hammered shackles from her seeping ankles,
vast land and seas were now the chains.

From sun up to sun down, my guide intoned,
*work, beatings, fighting for food -
just like the Great Hunger*, she laughed,
drifting softly towards the next room;
her finger traced the name of Mary Keogh,
imprisoned for ten years for stealing a hat.

I had to buy bread, she breathed in my ear.
Eighty hammocks crowded the third floor –
their faded fabric wefted with tears,
warped with repeating nightmares,
agonies shared by strong women
become children in the stinking dark.

Mary had married a ticket-of-leave man,
turned vile punishment into possibility.
yet she felt my sorrow at her dispossession
and her smile shivered down my arms.
Roots are inside, she said, vanishing
into a stark December afternoon -

on the still air I heard the jaunting
of fiddle, flute and drum.

Wine-dark Sea

Humpback

He cruises past the chilly shore,
a pebble's throw away,
glides by my tent again, a lover
looking up to see light in the window;
he blows fountains
in the face of doubts
over his warm-blooded sincerity.

Heaving his grey weight aloft,
like a jumbo jet at take-off,
he breaches in a shower of diamonds,
flashes his fluke at a still-light sky.
I can no longer resist his sighs;
catching me in a net of bubbles,
he plunges his barnacled head.

His slippery bulk soothes me
through currents of an iceberg sea,
I marvel at the might of baleen mouth,
agape with a tumult of small fry,
I feel him at ease with his power,
sense by finger tip his light wearing
of many million years' history.

Inflated with lung-bursting joy,
we surface to spout together,
through foam he dives once more,
leaving me in a pool of silence,
to envy Jonah his inner perspective.
Somewhere far off a pine-cone falls,
but only the humpback hears it.

The Net-shed

One whiff of the engine grease
fishermen spread, like lemon curd on toast,
I am a child in that refuge,
pebble-perched above a slope
spanned by groyne fingers.
I am peering seawards through
the net-shed window, crazed by cobwebs,
green waterproof ghosts overhead.

I am crouched in a draught with buoys
that jostle like party balloons,
inhaling the reek of wrecked fishboxes,
half-listening to rain rattle the tin roof.
Now I wind onto a bobbin the twine,
coarse and hairy as elephant hide,
knowing its fierce, tarry tang
will haunt me for days.

Grandad Chester, fishing patriarch,
who mends a net, silver-scaled still,
grunts for more twine; cracked fingers
thread, twist, pull, thread, twist, pull;
each knot, equidistant from the next,
despite his pale, faraway eyes,
his Inca information, recounting memories
of trawlers that plough phosphorus,

rebellious catches rending nets,
sips of enamel mug tea in storms.
Precise squares are frames in his life
of tidal rhythms and long perspectives.
He splices the double edge with corks,
weighted by stones with sea-worn holes,
the net heaps on others, a sleeping bear
in wait for the leap of shoals.

Heart of Oak

The beauty of wood,
colour, grain, sheen,
is celebrated by Weiwei;
his hands caress
dark density of ironwood,
trace huali's ghostly grain
with its delicate pear fragrance,
his face reflected
in African ebony's deep patina.

I recall the sweet smell of sawdust
at my father's work-place,
where he built clinker fishing boats
in traditional woods;
his square hands
ran over the stack of oak planks,
checking each for strength –
its 'heart' –
to choose for steaming
one to overlap precisely
the previous, riveted timber,
held fast by a mahogany keel.

My father never saw an art exhibition,
but he'd have appreciated
the accurate shaping,
artful, invisible joinery
of Weiwei's carpenters
and he'd want to stand small
among those mighty trees.
Yet unlike this artist, who risks
criticising a totalitarian regime,
my father never went to sea,
not even in the boats he built.

This Water

This water has no ending and no beginning: the words of Rose,
rescued from a sinking boat on the Mediterranean Sea, April 2015

this water -
is a slippery shape-shifter
spanning three continents,
nourishing a score of countries,
embracing numerous islands,
I'm Homer's *wine-dark sea:*
now smooth as Venetian glass
then my waves brawl and snarl

this water has no –
but don't blame me for shipwrecks,
moody Miss Moon hauls my currents
into her magnetic net -
yet those dreams of my azure ripples
rinsing golden sands of welcome
bait humans caught elsewhere
in a mesh of cruelty

this water has no ending -
moonless starless night
shrunken figures wade
crowd a rotten boat,
till the engine shivers into silence,
their Ark capsizes in a sea of despair
people are flotsam
and I hear their muezzin-like wails

this water has no ending and no –
I swaddle them awhile
then they sink softly
onto my patchwork bed
and long-dead sailors sing like seals
for those without names
whose shadows will sleep deep
among the silver shimmer of scales

this water has no ending and no beginning

Lobsters

As his sea-blue eyes meet mine,
I feel the pull of plaits
down my back,
his brow furrows
to focus
on my now much older face,
a twelve-mile horizon.

I remember the gold earring,
checked shirt,
ginger hairs bristling freckles
on sturdy-knuckled hands.
And for forty years,
I've borne his kindness
inside somewhere.

Daily combat with ocean
created in him
long distance views
on humanity,
salty wisdom,
wide-cast tenderness,
a generous net that trawled me,

helped a teenager face
an ongoing tide of family distress;
I've always connected that time
with a task he gave me:
tying lobsters' claws,
to prevent their cannibalism
in the store-pot.

Ana's View

Her legs refuse to get out of the car -
and the sandwich makes her nauseous
so she inhales scenic balm:
aquamarine stretching across the bay,
cut-out mountains pasted on a clean sky;
tourists throng the promenade below,
swimmers scream,
a pleasure boat throbs past.

She drags her leaden limbs out,
examines her faithful, red Fiat
(named Ana from the number-plate):
her peeling skin needs therapy, too,
rust along the door-sills
has metastasised to one wing,
the tyres are almost as bald
as the owner's head.

She struggles to lift the rear door,
garners a towel, beach-mat, faded sunhat
and discards them in a bin,
her limp body sags against hot metal
as she wipes sweat from her forehead
with a bony wrist;
in a final effort she cleans the windscreen
then locks Ana's doors.

Swifts squeal after insects
to welcome the dying of the day,
her car glows in the low sun
as if in remission; she says:
Ana, I'm leaving you now
with our favourite view,
while I go home to rust –

and she tosses the car-keys
into a sunset sea.

All at Sea

I used to build boats, you know.
This mantra throws a line ashore
to check his anchorless drifting
near unremembered coasts.
He doesn't know it
but he is mostly the father I knew
sociable, humorous
with flashes of causeless anger.

Eyes bright with innocence
peachy skin glowing over cheeks
small yet strong hands
persuade me of his presence.
Confusion masked by a smile
he asks my name again
politely
as though at the captain's table.

He surveys photos on the mantelpiece
a marooned sailor scanning the horizon
for the rescue boat.
I frame every sentence with *Dad*
but that word has become
a castaway, too.
He shakes his healthy shock of hair
like a dog reorganizing its ears.

He finds no clues in my face
so examines instead his shoes
from which he has again cut the laces.
Bought these in Portsmouth
during the war.
He fingers his buttonless cardigan
having taken against buttons, too.

To tell you the truth,
he laughs as though beginning a joke,
I have no idea where I am.
My hesitation allows him
to forget he ever wondered
and he's all at sea again –
too far out to see me wave.

Up Close and Personal

An unsure swimmer in strange seas,
I'm just relaxing muscles
in cold Galapagos water,
when a sleek pod-body
surfaces beside me
buoyant as an inflatable;
the sea-lion nudges me,
inviting admiration of her pup
that swims between us
with mittened hands
folded across the breast
in solemn prayer;
the baby nuzzles my fingers
while its wide-eyed gaze
wonders what I am;
the proud mother dives beneath me
spirals up the other side,
thrusts wiry whiskers close;
with calm certainty
her bulbous eyes examine me;
now the pup seeks her nipple
and they tumble below;
I tread water,
they re-appear metres away,
a maternal flipper raised skywards,
the warm suckling sound
drifts away
and I know my insignificance.

Scattering

Southern Queen is an Eastbourne pleasure boat, built in the 1950s by the poet's father. It still takes tourists to Beachy Head.

We climb the Peace Path
towards Beachy Head;
beside a tangle of bushes
Bob digs a hole -
not near the suicidal edge,
you'd be dizzy at the thought –
a fifty centimetre yew,
roots speckled with your particles,
braves the cliff-top breeze,
a robust *taxus baccata*
at ease in chalk,
symbol of death
and evergreen life.

The last time we were here
our final meeting,
you so old and frail
though a dozen years my junior,
addiction devouring your body,
tumbling your brain,
over the lunch you didn't eat
I spoke with my kid sister's ghost.

Remaining ashes smoke
over the snow-bright drop
swirl round a thermalling gull;
we wave at Dad,
phantom helmsman of the Southern Queen
as she pleasures tourists past the Head,
theirs a return trip.

On the train
I find the grit of you
under my nails
and ask tear-blurred trees,
like Peggy Lee,
Is that all there is?

Free Spirits

GALAPAGOS HERON

A hunched presence
deep in a vaulted cavern,
high priest of an obsidian cathedral;
bamboo stilt-legs rise
from a black rock platform,
a few loose feathers
shiver the edge of his smoky overcoat,
a sharp, yellow gaze glides
down the bladelike beak
ready to duel with its reflection,
his stillness born of aeons
waiting
watching.

Our dinghy close now,
he draws me into his meditation
on the quicksilver flicker of fish,
we both wonder about flight,
that slow, giant flap,
shaking dust from a fringed rug.

He flexes backward-bending knees,
trace of a shrug
then one foot is lifted,
replaced as if on eggshells
and his serenity
fills the cave of my heart.

The Pianist

A solemn Caribbean
slumped in a work jacket
with a beer at a corner table,
slides the glass to his right
stretches arms to free wrists
hands hover.

Across the sticky surface fingers ripple
the passion of Rachmaninov,
a wisp of smile
segues into Schubert, perhaps,
a delicate tempo
against the symphony
of syncopated tills
riffs of laughter
dissonance of TV football,
a flourish of arms to finish.

Scraping back his chair
he moves with a staccato rhythm
through to the Gents.
What is he?
Son of ambitious Jamaican parents?
Father a rail-worker
mother a nurse?

Back with the second pint,
a few sips
resumes recital,
modulating from soft sorrow
to lyrical pleasure,
maybe Satie then Mozart.

Is this Lewisham's Rain Man,
finding autistic consolation
in repetitive action?
Or a fugue
from some dreadful reality?
And that is his finale.

Arctic Trees

snow-clad
silver birch
pale
tall
slim
as Finns
rows of iced
Folies Bergère
dancers
offering
delicate
ostrich feathers
every breath
on pause

Nest

After winter at an inland yard
our boat moves to its offshore mooring
five miles as the crow flies.
A week later I find a nest on board,
balanced between the anchor's curve
and its green containing crate.

A perfect sphere of grass,
hairs, yellow unravelled string
wisps of black and white feathers
(a wagtail's nest, says Google);
inside, three blackened skeletons,
one beak open in a silent cry.

Next morning a sudden warble
from the boat's bow-rail -
a pied wagtail tilts her black cap
in coaxing song,
flexes wiry legs in a dance
to emphasize the plea.

Several days she comes,
then one evening with her partner,
dipping tails together;
he swoops twice over the crate -
a farewell fly-past
or surveying for a second nest?

Made me think of a woman
I met in Saigon,
who sent her two young sons
to safety in the United States
during the American War,
as the Vietnamese call it.

Ten years later,
a scrap of paper in her hand
with their last known address,
she searched the state, town, street,
found one fledgling
and took him home.

Buphagus

I could use an oxpecker,
a *buphagus* -
starling-like but less chatty -
to clear dandruff from my scalp
lift sleep from eye-corners
clean out ear-wax
beak dirt from under my nails
and between toes
peck along scaly heels
consume invisible parasites.

I might balk at letting him
near a cut finger
but once a year the full service,
an all-over nibble at dead skin;
and every day
I'd wear my scarlet beret
for my tickbird to perch on
when resting -
we'd be a sight for sore eyes
in Sainsbury's.

Wings

Gathering laundry from the line,
I find the rosemary bush
alive with the soft candle-flicker
of white butterflies,
tripping their light fantastic,
like ghostly arrhythmic hearts,
to the insistent hum of a few bees.

Drawn to the tiny tongues
of delicate mauve flowers,
they close their wings,
as if at prayer,
to sip sweetness;
when they brush to another bloom
spiky leaves waft warm scent
reminiscent of incense.

Now a pair spirals beyond the bush,
briefly flirting
before separation –
the kiss of eyelashes
blinking in the sun.

In this moment, I could believe,
as did the Ancient Greeks,
that butterflies are human souls
and wish my spirit
sported wings
as pure and joyous
as theirs.

Narcissus at the Window

Sharp rapping on a window
startles my afternoon:
smart, city banker of a bird –
puffed into his yellow waistcoat
under a blue, pin-striped jacket,
gelled black head with a stout beak
hammering the glass – hovers,
wings fluttering, sexy as long eyelashes,
tail fanned against the pane,
a miniature Venetian blind.

Then this great tit drops down,
curled feet clinging to the frame,
his partner offers supportive song
from a nearby lemon-tree,
her shrill tune unwinds
like a squeaky wheel,
draws from him a long fall of notes,
pearls unthreading from a string.

He attacks the glass again,
repeats the performance
at a second window;
then his bravura display appears
several days at most of our panes,
while I try not to surrender
to my Hitchcock moment.

Driven by competition,
desire to impress a mate
or narcissism,
he saw in the pool of our window
the handsomest tit around,
but the female didn't play rejected Echo –
they reared a full nest of chicks
in our garden wall.

Flower of Love

Move over, staid rose
bougainvillea will now be
the flower of love –

dance in narrow streets
clamber stone walls
smother high balconies

weave among sweet jasmine
a riot of exuberant colour:
scarlet, orange, magenta

cluster like origami wings
round a tiny white flower
guarded by fierce thorns

when veined petals fade
they will flutter to earth
sweet as *billets doux*

float skittishly down steps
skip into rustling corners
swirl indoors as free spirits

Happy Families

UDAIPUR PULSE

I thought you had just a bronchial cough,
till the doctor silked
into our hotel room,
pleated in a bright saree,
her two side-kicks,
stiff in white
bearing,
as if in a Hindu ceremony,
the sacred ECG machine.

My skin feels again the hot flush
that engulfed me,
as they wired you
to the oracle:
arrhythmia
         arrhythmia
                  arrhythmia
they chanted
and swept you away.

I don't remember speaking –
to ask where you were going
or even to say *Goodbye*.
I was helpless as Shiva
waving hundreds of arms
each with its own
unsteady
      pulse.

And hours later,
when you returned
nonchalantly,
slept naked beside me,
I watched your chest
through the night
rise and fall
        rise and fall
                rise and fall.

Folding Sheets

I loved going to the line on a blustery day,
watching sheets soar and belly
like pregnant sails on a galleon,
masted by the clothes-prop,
plying the suburban sea of trim lawns.
I'd bury my face in the winded linen,
inhale the mix of grass, blossom and smoke
overlaying the 'Persil Washes Whiter'.

Unpegged, sheets heaped in a plastic bowl
like mounds of whipped cream;
then came the pavan of folding:
first the preparation, like a curtsy,
a strong flap and gust of pulling it taut,
dangerous moments, when my mother
might jerk it from my uncertain grasp
and the fall onto the lino earn a scolding.

Now the dance of hands bringing together
the precise corners, so the half-sheet
hung between us like a snowdrift,
while the free hand gathered the lower edge
to bring the cloth flat once more;
after a second fold we glided forward,
meeting centre, where I took my mother's end
from fingers with ugly, swollen knuckles.

Then she slid hands down each side to mid-way,
I released my grip, she halved the length again,
sighing it over her stomach. One more doubling,
before the sheet augmented the ironing pile.
Years later I discovered I had learned to fold
in her particular way, left-handedly, making me
a clumsy companion in stowing sails,
packing the tent, or storing a stage floorcloth.

And now, when I iron my sheets,
folded without help,
I see the arthritic joints of my left hand.

Forgetting the Lines

Old age is endless rehearsals,
groping for words, sense
and fluency,
unable to weave them
into meaningful dialogue.

So senility must be
every actor's nightmare -
'drying' on stage,
caught open-mouthed
in a spotlight.

The mind empties
like a post-show theatre,
saddened by remnants
of make-up
mislaid props
faded curtains
and dust
that once danced in the limelight,
now sinking
onto blank stage-canvas.

The backstage mirror shows
my unknowable face,
with tears on its cheeks –
are they real
or glycerine?

Close the tabs, someone,
start the music,
slow fade to black,
open the grave-trap,
move over, Yorick!

Offbeat Concerto

White coats and soft shoes rhythm past
        suited consultant flaps a folder
disappears into swishing lift
re-appears   strides towards pale distance.
        Background Bach counterpoints
      racing, uncertain hearts
                    as soloists gather to tune up.
A Harrods bag rustles against confident pinstripes
pausing   to listen outside consecutive rooms.
      An elderly hand-knitted sweater, leaning over a stick
gasps onto a waiting chair.
        A denim jacket carries the score
                  arrhythmia notated on a
          cardiogram.
        Pregnant dungarees sway on clacking heels
walking the tightrope between life and   death.

Mrs Sandra Clark! intones a loud voice
accusing silence   followed by a slam.
Scratching pens fill in forms, hovering over   'next-of-kin'
        couples touch at elbow or knee
brave lips murmuring cold comfort
        continuous sibilance of turning newspapers
            syncopated by timid knocks on doors.
In time with a violin *diminuendo* (*Night on the Bare Mountain* now)
a breathless woman subsides onto creaking bench
                        rummages a noisy bag
retrieves from the floor her collapsed coat.
Mrs Sandra Clark?   She shambles away

    as my partner is called down the corridor.
        I'm left inhaling air dense with mortality.
Drums pulse in my ears droned by coughs, shuffles, sighs.
        Fleeting smiles mask unwanted thoughts
we shrink to our child selves   naked   equal
        facing the music.
Mrs Clark emerges in tears   trailing the coat.
Impassive faces averted.
        Several hushed beats.

Concealing our almost good news we fugue across silent carpet
dance over pavement   cracks   to the throb of traffic.

Happy Families

When I was eight and wore long plaits,
I would scamper the dark distance
from her wicker gate to brown-painted door,
whispering fir-trees and prickly bushes
grabbing at me on the uneven path;
Miss Mear was spindly as her pines
her face severe in repose, angelic in action.

Every Saturday she welcomed a knot of girls
to learn the faded art of hand-sewing;
we huddled near a fire that popped and hissed,
stitching reluctant hems and wayward patches,
while she sewed, with her strangely large hands,
exquisite miniature dolls, wearing cloth faces,
golden hair and silk-thread smiles.

Our tasks passing muster, the reward was
a hard fought game of 'Happy Families',
the names and professions on these cards
re-conjuring Miss Mear's genteel childhood;
before leaving we were allowed to peep
into her tiny doll's house, a Lilliputian world,
peopled by her imperceptible stitches.

One week I scurried early up her path
to find her lying unconscious by the door
one bony hand at a right angle to its wrist;
when I visited her in the nursing home,
she pressed gently into my palm a tiny doll
with black wool plaits, in her own armchair,
carefully sewing a fine seam.

And then I knew
that we ungrateful girls
had been Miss Mear's happy family.

Mimosa

This morning our garden mimosa
stole my heartbeat
with its yellow fountain
of tumbling exuberance.

Its flowers arrive as tiny balls
spiralling the stem
among fern-like sprays
of leafy symmetry.

Slowly buds unfold
dangle their profusion
of fluffy filaments
till a Seurat *pointilliste* painting
dances a blur before my eyes.

But mimosas along the shore
keep their larger balls closed
as if to resist
fierce black thorns
that guard the wild tree;
in compensation
they bounce sweet perfume
into my face.

And I am a child
fingers on my mother's scent-bottle
silver top pierced by a tube
leading to a rubber bulb – one squeeze
and air pulses
with that haunting aroma.

Sunday Stones

A freckled child skips
along the gravelled path
of weekly pilgrimage,
parental tread in pursuit
round the Sussex-flint church
among elms swaying with rooks,
between *Dearly Beloved*
and *In Loving Memory,*
past granite figures' outstretched arms,
rain-stained crosses,
mossed carvings of angels,
to reach
the small, marble-framed plot.

She wrinkles her nose at rotting stalks,
rubs bird-lime from the headstone
with a careless sleeve,
wanders away from the family ritual
of cossetting
her brother's recent grave,
to feed hand-plucked grass
over the fence.

The horse whinnies
as she teeters down a sloping plank
over the pebble-filled ditch
between graveyard
and beckoning field.

STUFF

Home at midnight
unlock the door
cold draught through a forced window -
from a gaping wardrobe
a *favela* mudslide of garments
flows onto the floor,
coats and jackets jumble in a doorway
as if dropped by fleeing refugees,
separated shoes, mixed with scarves,
black underwear, rolled socks,
tumble in a random heap,
wait for Cambodian children to scavenge;
drawers surrender liquorice allsort contents:
papers, blunt pencils, keys, a hussif,
cough sweets, odd foreign coins;
sheets in the raided linen-chest
grumble at the disturbance of piled order,
beat-up cushions crouch under the sofa,
a violated set of Babushka dolls
scatters in halves across a table,
chairs are silent witnesses;
the insistent lure of a hidden stash of cash
leads to up-turned mattresses,
books parted on shelves,
each box, tin, bag undone, unlidded or unzipped,
kitchen cupboards rummaged,
even the cooker-hood filters removed;
but it's a poor haul
from the flotsam and jetsam of our lives:
a few Australian dollars
and a plastic bag of cheap earrings;
Reason not the need, says Lear,
yet we must:
what is this voracious appetite for stuff?
As if possessions alleviate loneliness,
compensate for failure,
usurp death?
Now bars on windows will declare to all
that the inmates of this asylum
have too much stuff.

www.ingramcontent.com/pod-product-compliance
Lightning Source LLC
Chambersburg PA
CBHW042130100526
44587CB00026B/4248